Your Best College Guide

What Top Students Know About
Making A's and Landing Jobs

By Cody Smith

Disclaimer Notice:

Please note the information contained within this document is for educational and entertainment purposes only. All effort has been executed to present accurate, up to date, and reliable, complete information. No warranties of any kind are declared or implied. Readers acknowledge that the author is not engaging in the rendering of legal, financial, medical or professional advice. The content within this book has been derived from various sources. Please consult a licensed professional before attempting any techniques outlined in this book.

By reading this document, the reader agrees that under no circumstances is the author responsible for any losses, direct or indirect, which are incurred as a result of the use of the information contained within this document, including, but not limited to, — errors, omissions, or inaccuracies.

Dedication

This book is dedicated to Tom Peyton.

Little did I know our brief conversation would change the trajectory of my approach to college. Who knew it would later help me write this book? Who knows how it will help in the future?

I am grateful for the time I got to spend with you before you passed on.

Rest in peace.

Table of Contents—The Syllabus

Do **<u>NOT</u>** continue reading the book before grabbing a copy of my collection of 127+ FREE online resources for college students. . .

you will regret it!

http://rebrand.ly/collegeresources

As a thank you for getting a copy of the book, I want to share with you my collection of 127+ college resources.

With it your friends will wonder:

- How you get your assignments done so quickly?
- Why you seem so confident going into interviews?
- How you stay effortlessly organized?
- Why your resume looks like a professional team put it together?
- How you study less yet make better grades?
- And so much more!

The best part? I'm continuously adding to it when I come across great resources that need to be added to the list.

>> Go here: http://rebrand.ly/collegeresources to get instant access to my list of 127+ college resources!

Introduction—Student Orientation

Ah college: the place where adulting begins. College comes into most people's lives at such an odd time. For the most part, it's for kids fresh out of high school and finally out of eyesight and arm's length of hovering parents, who probably made the majority of the decisions for them.

Depending on how structured your life was growing up, you were probably told to eat, to go to school, to act and behave a certain way, to be home by a certain time, to go to bed before too late, to brush your teeth, to do chores around the house before you could hang out, to not rot your brain out too much with video games, to date people they approved of, and to stop locking your bedroom door.

Then suddenly you go off to college and no one is telling you what to do anymore, though some parents may still try. For some new college students, having all this newfound freedom and power to decide how to live their life is exhilarating and awesome. For others, not having that guidance and structure in place they once had under the tutelage of their parents is terrifying and uncomfortable.

You can decide to stay up all night, to eat nothing but Lucky Charms cereal, to pay attention to personal hygiene or not, or to binge watch the entire *Mad Men* series instead of going to your English Composition class.

Not to mention the classroom environment is completely different from what you experienced in high school. Professors couldn't care less if you pay attention, if you pass the class, or if you even show up at all. Some professors will speak terrible English, like you're on a crappy tour guide through a calculus jungle in a foreign country. The only catch is at the end of the tour, you'll be expected and fully responsible to pass a test on information your tour guide shouted during the tour. If you don't pass, you get to pay more money to take the crappy tour guide again.

Yay . . .

This is what makes the transition from high school to

college so tough. Not only are you on your own to figuring out this whole adult thing, you're also juggling educating yourself in a system that couldn't care less if you pass or fail. On top of that, regardless if you even gradate, you'll still have to find a way to pay for all of it.

Everything is 100 percent on you.

Is this a bad thing? No.

Is it easy? Double no.

This is why I decided to write this book: to provide insight into the college scene from a guy who has been in your shoes, got spanked by a challenging engineering curriculum, found a way to spank college back, and did it in a way that allowed me to exit college debt free and with the job I actually wanted.

To be frank, many books and guides on college deal with all sorts of topics, like dealing with psycho roommates that think bugs speak to them, navigating co-ed dorms, dating, dealing with being handed a beer along with a gallon of milk at parties, and all sorts of others stuff.

This book is strictly covering the education piece to help get you to graduation (the first half of the book), and how to actually land the job in your career field (the second half of the book) instead of winding up being a college-educated, minimum-wage earning Macy's employee, wondering what went wrong.

I'll show you how to play your cards right to walk out of college debt free and with a plump resume to separate you from everyone else gunning for jobs.

In short, I'll show you how to not suck at college.

It doesn't matter if you're just starting out in college, whether you're about to graduating wondering what comes next or somewhere in the middle, this book has something for you.

Interested?

Good.

Read on.

Treat College like a Full-time Job

If you're like me, then you almost expected college to be similar to high school: a full day of class followed by an afternoon full of homework. Why would you expect anything less? That's exactly how it's been your whole life up until that point.

I was pleasantly surprised to have just a handful of classes a day, sometimes none, and I'd finish all my assignments before lunch.

When I first started college, I was a model student: I was early to classes, sat in the front, completed assignments early, studied throughout the week, woke up around six a.m., went to bed early, and didn't party on weekends.

That lasted a total of six weeks. Gradually, I figured out what classes I needed to pay attention to and which ones I could sleep in or not show up at all.

Assignments got pushed off to right before they were

due, and studying throughout the week turned into cramming the night before or the morning of an exam.

Weekends became time to party, recovering the next morning while regretting going too hard the night before, swearing I'd never do it again, followed by partying the next weekend.

Staying up late felt natural and sleeping in was glorious.

My world revolved around maximizing pleasure and minimizing pain. While that tends to be the goal for most human beings, college students tend to go about it in the most unhealthy and unproductive of fashions. We value getting the highest grades, with the least amount of effort, while loading up on the most amount of fun and pleasure as possible. More often than not, the "highest grade" is replaced with whatever grade is needed to pass and eventually graduate.

It's easy to assume we're being the most efficient with our time and effort by going with the minimum required route, though that is seldom ever the case.

Let's say two students in an accounting 101 class approach the class differently. One student skips every other class because attendance is not part of the grade; completes assignments the day they are due; crams before a test, pulling an all-nighter; knowledge barfs all over the test; then makes an A in the class.

The other student shows up to every class, completes assignments the day they are assigned, studies and reviews materials gradually over the semester, does not have to pull all-nighters before tests, then comes out with an A at the end of the semester.

Question: Are the two As equal?

Based on a GPA, they are weighted the exact same. However, the input that went into the grade and what remains afterward is completely different.

It all boils down to knowledge retention: how much of what you learned over the semester will stick around in memory long after the semester is over. This is dependent on whether your retained what you learned in long-term memory and how easily it can be recalled.

Let's say every time you receive a piece of need-to-know information is like planting a tree somewhere in the forest, which is the inner workings of your brain. Let's say you went to class and were lectured on a topic in history for about an hour and you took notes.

At this point, you've gone over the material once and for long enough that it's made its way to long-term memory. This new material then is like a baby tree that you carried deep into the woods and planted around other trees just like it. Afterward, you leave and forget about it.

Fast forward to the night before the test. You haven't touched the material since the day in class. You try to recall the information, but you can't. The path you took to carry the tree has grown over and you can't find your way back nor recall the information. And the baby tree, since you didn't take time to regularly water it, has dried up and died. What's left behind is a sad remnant of its formal self, which makes reviewing the material familiar, but you're practically starting from square one.

Now when you cram for the test, you're replacing that memory with another (replacing the old tree with multiple little ones), which will hopefully live long enough for the test, but it won't last much longer than that.

Not only are you wasting time relearning material, but chances are, you're going to quickly forget what you learned again!

Lastly, if you are cramming for a test, meaning you are reviewing several classes' worth of material at one time, you're basically trying to carrying multiple baby trees into the woods to plant. With cramming, you're trying to remember and recall a lot of information over a short period of time. That makes for a lot of baby trees, and a long time to carry each one deep into the forest, forcing you to stay up late.

Hours later, late into the night and early morning when you've crammed enough, all your baby trees are finally planted. You dump your leftover energy drink or coffee that got you through the long night to water the trees.

The baby trees will make it through the night so they will be alive for the test. Since you spent so long carrying the trees through the woods, you know the trail to get back to the trees pretty well and can recall a good portion of the information. However, since the roots haven't taken root and you most likely will not review the information again after the exam, the trees will eventually die and the trail will grow over once again.

Let's compare that to a different scenario.

The day after you were lectured on the material, you pulled out the notes you took and transferred them to a separate notebook that you will use for review when it comes time for the test. Transferring the notes helps you review the material again, which reinforces that information in your memory. This is like watering the tree, using the same trail you used the day before to plant the tree. Now it's got a fighting chance of living and growing.

Then, on the way to class, you recall the information by talking out loud, rehearsing the material as best you can. This helps build the connection from a barely marked path (a place in your memory) to a well-maintained information highway leading to quick information recall.

You repeat this periodically throughout the semester as you regularly revisit the tree and water it. Thus, the tree continues to grow as you learn more about the subject. You can easily recall the information since the path to get to the tree is well-maintained and quick. All of these aspects work together, helping your memory last for a very long time after the class is over.

By the time you are given your final exam, you simply do another review to recall the information you've learned over the semester the week of the test.

Meanwhile, everyone else is up late, cramming information they had long forgotten, consuming copious amounts of Top Ramen and Red Bull. Instead, you're happily asleep, stress free, and about as worried about the test as you are about what you're going to eat for breakfast.

Those are two completely different worlds! Two opposite approaches to studying in college. One is miserable and inefficient; the other, beneficial and peaceful. You get to choose how your college career plays out.

Choosing to study in this fashion rather than cramming has far-reaching benefits beyond a stress-free semester and a good GPA. This form of gradual review, recall, and reinforcement of new information becomes increasingly more important as classes and information start to stack on top of each other. This holds true for just about any class related to your major.

For example, if you are going for a technical degree,

you will most likely take calculus one through four. What you learn in Calculus I will be the foundation for what you learn in Calculus II, III and IV. Having truly learned the material in the first class and being able to recall the information quickly will benefit you greatly in the classes to come.

It doesn't stop there. As you progress through your curriculum, leading up to your more advanced classes in your junior and senior year, not only does your classwork stack onto each other, but the information will be heavily interconnected and woven together to create the bigger picture necessary to start a career in whatever you have decided to major in.

Had you been cramming this entire time, you would have gaps in knowledge you once had (but not for very long) but was never reinforced. Thus, the tree you planted never got what it needed to thrive. Now you either have to use up precious time to relearn the concepts and information you had forgotten or hope it wasn't critical and your grades won't drop because of it.

But why? Why spend so much money, time, and effort learning just so it can be quickly forgotten? Just so you can get by? Just so you can get a degree with the least amount of effort? Because obviously everyone who gets a college degree gets a job in their field, right?

Wrong.

The statistics are staggering. According to a report by the Strada Institute, 43 percent of graduates end up underemployed ("The Permanent Detour", 2018), meaning they took a job that didn't require they have a four-year degree.

Trying to get a degree with the least amount of effort gets you an expensive piece of paper with the least amount of knowledge backing it up.

On its own, your diploma has zero value. None. Its value is strictly from the knowledge you received and retained in your major, not from the name of the school that's printed on it, not from the signature of the college president who signed it, and certainly not from the gold insignia that tends to be on all of them.

Its value comes from you. Only you.

Many may disagree with me, but I don't care. They may say the degree gets you your first job (if you get your first job), and then from there, you'll learn the needed information. But what if your first job isn't even in your career field?

And even if you do get a job that requires your degree, if you've spent the last four years putting in the least amount of effort to get your degree, what makes you think you'll do any different once you get a job? What skills do you really have?

You spent four years getting really good at getting by and being lazy instead of really learning the fundamentals of your major. Yes, lazy. Cramming is lazy, inefficient, and a waste of time. But somehow, we, as college students, have convinced ourselves that cramming and all-nighters are a part of the college experience and an acceptable form of study. However, it doesn't have to be that way, and just because the majority decide to wait until the last minute and cram doesn't mean that's the best route. Far from it.

I know I sound high and mighty, but I know all of this from experience. I fell into the world of cramming and all-nighters mainly because it was too easy to put off studying assignments until the last minute. Sleeping in, goofing off, and binge-watching Netflix seemed more important than school.

I also easily disguised my procrastination with statements like "I work better under pressure," giving meaning and value to putting off what could be done today.

When I continued to make good grades, I took that as a sign that this was the correct approach. But as my classes became increasingly more technical, difficult, and demanding, I noticed the error in my belief and started to lose confidence in my study strategy.

The material became increasingly more difficult to understand and not just because the concepts were advanced. I simply could not remember all the fundamental concepts needed to understand the new material.

Since I crammed for all of the prerequisites classes, I didn't retain the material. And I needed to know this material for my advanced classes.

Now all the free time I had cherished got eaten alive from having to go back and relearn old information, trying to put all the pieces together before the first test.

I struggled a ton that semester, but I learned just how stupid cramming really was, and I knew I needed to fix my studying habits, but I really was not sure how I to go about it. I had been cramming just about my entire college career so I didn't know what else to do.

Over Christmas break, after the semester where my efforts as a crammer were catching up to me, I spent some time with a good friend of mine from high school who I hadn't seen much since we graduated. We were at his house hanging out when his dad popped into the kitchen to say hello. We chatted a little bit about how college was going.

"I'm struggling," I told him. "My classes are getting tough," I continued, though that wasn't the only reason for my struggle.

He smirked and had a look on his face like he just relived some memories from his own experience in college years prior.

"You're not cramming, are you?" He said bluntly still smirking. His question caught me off guard and pierced me like a knife as if he could read my thoughts. I just stared back at him for what felt like an eternity, feeling like I had just got caught telling a lie. I merely nodded in agreement.

"Yeah, I remember those days. I did the same until I started treating college like a full-time job."

"A full-time job?"

"Yep, like a full-time job. During the week when I wasn't in classes, I would be in the library either working on assignments, studying, or reviewing from nine to five. My evenings and weekends were mine to do however I pleased, and my college experience thereafter became less stressful and more enjoyable."

It seemed like a terrible idea at first, but I couldn't stop thinking about our conversation days after. The more I thought about it, the more it started to make perfect sense.

We don't go to college with the goal to party, have fun, and goof off without parent supervision. Our goal with college is to prepare ourselves to eventually get a job. Why not treat college like a job in preparation for that ultimate goal?

The next semester, I decided to take what my friend's dad said to heart: I started treating college like a full-time job.

Before I was enjoying sleeping in until just shy of the amount of time it took to fly out of bed and get to class, only attending classes if I thought I truly needed to, and completing the minimum amount of assignments I had to get done while procrastinating and pushing the rest off until the weekend (Sunday night). I had a chronic "I'll get it done tomorrow" mentality along with most of my peers.

I wasted my free time throughout the day on goofing off, Netflix, YouTube videos, hanging out with friends, roaming the internet, scrolling through social media, sleeping, hanging out at the fraternity house, or just about anything to distract myself from what I actually needed to get done.

The first thing that had to go was my mentality that free time was my first priority. Instead, I was going to fill my day with completing assignments and studying when I wasn't in class, treating my education like a nine–five job.

To do that, I had to stop staying up to two a.m. and waking up at ten a.m. Fixing that was not going to be a gradual thing. I needed to rip the Band-Aid off as fast as possible. So to adjust my sleep cycle, I went all in. The first day of classes that next semester I woke up at four a.m., pulling in two hours of sleep. I trudged through the day resisting the never-ceasing temptation to nap and crashed at eight p.m. and woke up at five a.m. the next morning.

I gradually settled at waking up at six a.m. and going to bed at ten p.m., regardless if it was a weekday or weekend. Was that the best way to change my sleep cycle? Probably not, but it worked for me, though it took a good week to settle into my new sleep cycle and probably a month to get over the temptation to sleep in over the weekend.

With my sleep cycle in check, I could now fill my days with assignments and studying. I would get to campus at seven a.m., find a spot in our study lounge, and park myself there until my first class.

In between classes, I would either work on a homework assignment or study or review material that I had already gone over in class. Then around four p.m. through the rest of the evening, I could do whatever I wanted.

At first, I hated it. There were so many things I would

have rather been doing, but I stuck with it and I'm glad I did. After a few short weeks of my new approach, I was much less stressed out and life was good.

The real change happened when my first test came around, and I didn't need to study or look at the material the week of the test. Because I had been studying and reviewing the past several weeks, I knew the material inside and out. It was a complete change from the semesters before.

Then something weird happened.

I was running out of things to do . . .

I quickly became ahead on all my assignments and after a while, my studying and reviewing were offering diminishing returns, which was to be expected. It was at that moment I realized it didn't take much time or effort to get everything done. It was surprising how much easier my course load had become.

That semester, I also took one of the more difficult classes in our electrical engineering curriculum: high power transmissions and distributions. I had talked to other students who had taken the class the prior semester and they summed up the class in one word: brutal.

They were right.

That class was brutal. The material was tough to pick up, the homework was tough to do, and the tests were no different.

Still, my strategy proved advantageous. I had been studying and reviewing for several weeks. By the time the week of the first test had come around, I couldn't have cared less about studying for it. Instead, I spent my extra time teaching other students the material who needed help studying.

When you get to the point that you can confidently teach other people the class material, you know you're ready for the test.

Test day felt like any other day of class, which is huge coming from a guy who suffered from test anxiety. In the past, I would shake and sweat before the professor passed out the test. Then I would brain dump everything I had crammed over the past twenty-four–forty-eight hours, and I would usually be one of the last ones still taking the test.

This new strategy had completely flipped the switch on my test anxiety. When I crammed, just thinking about the test gave me anxiety, causing me to push off studying even more, whereas my new strategy had me studying so far in advance that the test wasn't even on my radar. I didn't have a sense of anxiety when I studied and neither did I on the day of the test.

Since I had reviewed and quizzed myself on the material consistently, my recall of the information was incredibly fast while taking the test. It took me thirteen minutes to finish, and when I turned in my test, my professor thought I had accepted defeat, signed my name at the top, and turned it in without even trying.

After the test, I went back to the study lounge and started working on other assignments and studying for other classes. In the past, I would have gone straight home and passed out from staying up all night and skipped the rest of the classes I had that day.

The next week we got our test, and before passing them back to us, he told us the average grade was a thirty-three. That was a gut check. The entire class, including me, figured we had all failed the test.

He then said, "I will add a curve to the test based on the highest score." Hearing that resulted in a united sigh of relief. We figured with an average of a thirty-three, the highest score was probably around fifty. You could taste the hope in the room. Someone in the front of the room looked back at everyone and said so everyone could hear, "I hope you all failed miserably." Everyone chuckled from his comment as the professor started passing back the tests.

The professor said, "Go ahead and add fourteen points to the grade written at the top of your test. That is the curve."

Fourteen points?! That's it? That means some dangus

scored an eighty-six on the test . . .

. . . I was the dangus.

As soon as I saw it, I tried hiding it, but the guy beside me saw my grade and blurted out, "Oh gosh, it was you!"

I now had everyone's attention. The whole class was practically grumbling in disapproval of my high score. I had betrayed my people and brought much dishonor to my peers.

It's not easy crushing the hopes and dreams of all of your peers in a matter of seconds, though who truly cared what they thought of me. What I knew for sure was that my new approach worked.

And in the end, did I really have test anxiety, or did I just never put enough time and effort to properly prepare?

I give this example to illustrate my point, not to brag. Was I smarter than everyone in my class? Absolutely not. I just studied and reviewed the material more consistently than everyone else, though not necessarily for longer than anyone else. That was the key to my success.

Unfortunately, old habits die hard. After having the most successful semester of my college career, I hit summer break. It was the first summer that I didn't have a class or an internship, so I decided to take a break and relax over the summer. I slept in, lounged around, was very unproductive, and I was lovin' it.

However, that behavior carried over into the next semester and I fell right back into my old ways. Sleeping in, staying up late, procrastinating, cramming for a test, and prioritizing free time. I'd forgotten all about treating college like a job and I was reaping the consequences: I was stressed out again and because I wasn't fully committing the new material to memory, my test anxiety came back.

I remember cramming for a test at three in the morning halfway through the semester when I finally decided to switch back to treating college like a job again. Soon after, I caught back up and things had settled back down like they were the semester before.

To make sure that didn't happen again next semester, I used https://www.futureme.org to send myself an email that would arrive in my email box on the first day of class the following semester. I had completely forgotten about it and chuckled a bit when I received it. The email read:

Don't be a dangus!

Treat it like a full-time job.

-C

P.S. Send wife flowers. There is a good chance you haven't done that in months

Sadly, I completely forgot over Christmas break and needed the reminder.

The rest of this chapter contains tips and strategies to make your transition to treating college like a full-time job as smooth as possibly. The more strategies you implement, the more efficient you'll become with your time. Applied correctly, your full-time job will start to look more like a part-time job.

Know your preferred study environment

Everyone has a preferred environment that helps them study, and it's beneficial to know yours. I wish I could study and get assignments done at home so I could mosey out of bed, crack open my laptop on my couch, and get to work with a giant bowl of fruit loops . . . but I can't. I can't focus on assignments or studying in my own castle, and I hardly get anything done.

I also know I work faster and am more productive around people who are also working—preferably people I don't know. I freakin' love to talk, so I can easily kill an hour of my time striking up a conversation with someone I know. So I'll usually choose a library or coffee shop to get work done since I likely won't run into someone I know.

Additionally, I work better when I'm not cold. Our study lounge in our college building was either freezing or toasty hot. On the days it was cold, I'd go somewhere else to work. When I'm cold, I can't focus on anything. I want to do nothing else but stay warm, move, shuffle, breathe into my cold, cupped hands, etc. I can't get anything accomplished when 90 percent of my thoughts are "Good gracious, it's cold. Why is it so cold? How do I not be cold?!" Being hot doesn't affect me nearly as much.

Take some time and effort to discover your best study environment and stick to it and tweak it as you go. It took me a few weeks to nail down my preferred study environment. Knowing that also helped me complete all of my books, which are mainly handwritten in a warm coffee shop.

Know your best way to learn

One of my best friends Tyler can just be present in class and fully grasp the material. He's doesn't have to take notes, he doesn't have to review material, and he doesn't have to complete homework assignments to understand or comprehend new information. Shoot, he doesn't even need to be awake in class, and somehow, he still earns As.

Yeah, he's one of *those* people.

Meanwhile, I'm feverishly taking notes, rewriting notes afterward to help me study, making flash cards, and quizzing myself for who knows how long to fully grasp the lesson.

Makes me sick!

People learn material differently. Some people can watch a demonstration and pick it up perfectly, while others need to hear how a task is done before fully grasping an idea.

Some need to be more hands-on; others, simply read about it and learn that way, while others might need to talk about the lesson to put all the pieces together.

Knowing how you learn can save you an incredible amount of time and frustration. If you're a visual learner but you're trying to learn something orally, it could take you a lot longer to understand the material.

I wish schools would put effort into helping students discover their strengths and weaknesses when it comes to their learning style, but they don't. It's completely up to you to find out.

I'm a tactile learner. I need to physically do something to fully understand the information I'm trying to learn. Thus, I take a massive amount of notes during lectures. If I just sit there and listen, I'll hardly remember a thing. I have to take notes and I have to work out examples.

Secondly, I learn visually. This isn't as crucial as physical learning, but it's certainly second best.

With orally learning, I'm practically useless. It's pathetic how much I forget when I just try to listen. Just listening drains me of energy, sucking me dry. Physical learning, on the other hand, does the exact opposite. I can get energy from it.

You can tell what your learning style is by the amount of resistance you face during it.

Most people have a dominant and secondary learning style. Your dominant is your go-to, but you can create some synergy by combining your learning styles to better grasp the material.

If your dominant style is auditory with a secondary style of visual learning, you can easily combine the two styles by listening during the lecture and then talking with someone or out loud to yourself about what you just learned.

The key is learning how to convert a professors' teaching style into one that best suits yours. Ryan Blair, the author of *Nothing to Lose, Everything to Gain: How I Went From Gang Member to Multimillionaire*

Entrepreneur, talks about how he really struggled in school until he learned he was an auditory learner. He started taking a tape recorder to class, recorded the lessons, and then listened to the recordings later so he could better comprehend and remember the material.

Let's say your professor's teaching style involves PowerPoint slides with huge blocks of text, which they will spend most of the time reading verbatim as if you are illiterate. Meanwhile your learning style is predominantly visual, adding a layer of difficulty to your comprehension of what is being taught. To compensate, you'll want to change the format of the material to suit your needs. Converting the material will take some extra work on your part since the professor won't do it for you, but it will be well worth it in the end.

The first thing you'll want to do may sound a little drastic but hang with me. You'll want to actually open the text book you purchased for the class. Sounds crazy, I know, but you might as well get your money's worth for how much those things cost. Odds are your textbook already has graphics or visual analogies to further illustrate a concept or material to help you learn and comprehend it.

I don't know why, but students seem to have this unspoken rule that you don't actually read or ever use the textbook assigned for a class. You just buy them because it's required, gripe about how crazy expensive they are, and hope you'll get anywhere close to what you paid for them when the semester is over when you try to sell it back to the bookstore.

I believe this comes from an expectation that everything you need to know will be addressed during class since high school was that way. In reality, what you learn in class is simply the basics and you are expected to go deeper into the material outside of class to further grasp the material, using the textbook as a starting point. The textbook is there to assist you in your learning.

If your class was not assigned a textbook or you are still

y understanding what you learned in class from the textbook, I recommending turning to good ole YouTube. YouTube is great place to learn a concept or lesson visually simply by searching for it on the website. This has certainly saved my bacon several times in my electrical engineering classes. Electrical engineering is called black magic engineering by the other engineering disciplines simply because you can't quite see what's happening. This really sucked for a tangible and visual learner such as myself. I turned to YouTube to find someone who took the time to make a visual representation of what I was learning in class.

Like I said earlier, it will take some time and effort to find your learning style and how to work with material that is in a different format. The earlier you learn how, the better off you'll be down the road when your classes get increasingly more difficult.

Guard your workday with strict discipline

If you decide to leave behind the days of procrastination and sleepless nights filled with last-minute studying for a test, you will need to guard your time with strict discipline; otherwise, you can easily fall back into your old ways.

I marked the hours between seven a.m. and four p.m. Monday through Thursday, and between seven a.m. and one p.m. on Fridays as dedicated workday time. In between class, I was either working on homework or studying. That's it.

Afterward, my evenings and weekends were mine to do as I pleased. It all sounds so simple, and yet it can be very difficult to stick to it. You must become a dictator of your time and guard it with earnest effort. Because the moment you don't, your time is no longer yours; it is now someone (or something) else's.

When you first start to treat your time in college as a full-time job, you will meet resistance. The world does not like it when you take time for only yourself. The world will do whatever it can to get a piece of it. It knows if it can advance an inch, it will take a mile.

What I mean by "the world" is anything outside of homework or studying that takes up your time: scrolling through Facebook and YouTube videos; replying to emails, Reddit, and text messages; engaging in phone calls with your mother and conversations with others not related to homework or studying; petting your cat; daydreaming; receiving phone notifications; watching T.V. and Netflix; sleeping; browsing the internet; attending campus events; playing sports; hanging out with friends; snacking; attending clubs; participating in intramurals, fraternity or sorority functions, and meetings; or picking your nose.

Distractions are everywhere, and they will take up your time, but only if you let them.

You know your vices, or at least you think you do. I certainly thought I did until I started treating college like a full-time job. I thought I had a good handle on staying focused, but I was sadly mistaken. When I was studying or working on an assignment that didn't interest me, I would repeatedly stare off into space and daydream for several minutes. After I would snap back out of it, I'd instinctively check my phone for any notifications, stumble onto Facebook, scroll through my feed for twenty minutes, then feel worse about myself because my life seemed so boring and unfulfilled compared to all my friends on Facebook. Hopefully, by then, I would realize how much time I wasted and get to work, but not always. So something had to change, or nothing was going to work out.

Sometimes you think you have guarded your time well and feel accomplished after four hours of "working", but it's later in the day and you realize you didn't get much actual work down. You didn't realize you spent twenty minutes texting friends. You forgot about the three trips to the bathroom, and on one of those trips, you had a twenty-minute debate over some trivial sports game you watched over the weekend. You didn't account for the time spent cleaning out your desk and backpack, which you had been neglecting and compared to actually doing homework or studying, tidying up felt more important and satisfying to get done.

Replying to one message on Facebook resulted in an endless scroll through your feed before taking a left turn into Reddit, which somehow got you lost watching video after video of Vine compilations on YouTube.

You didn't feel the hour slip by going through your emails, formulating a response, and responding to each one. Somehow taking care of other people's to-do list got a higher priority than taking care of your own.

It's no wonder we can't get anything done. We have to be really intentional with our time. Otherwise, we put trivial tasks and to-do items that we find more interesting or that are easier to accomplish on a higher priority compared to more pressing, uninteresting, harder to accomplish to-do tasks.

I started turning my phone on airplane mode and stopped answering text messages, emails, and phone calls completely during this time. If anyone did strike up a conversation with me, I ended it quickly if they didn't need anything from me, by saying, "I've really got to finish this. Do you mind if we talk later?" and that usually did the trick.

Any meetings that needed to be scheduled, for whatever reason, I requested they be during lunch or during the evenings; otherwise, I would just ask that the meeting minutes be sent to my email.

I used a free web extension called WasteNoTime that works for both Chrome and Safari. This app allows you to restrict certain websites that notoriously take up a lot of your time and gives you a report on how much time you spend on sites such as Facebook, YouTube, etc.

If you use Firefox, use LeechBlock NG.

But what about smartphones?

We can't forget about those time sucks. Yes, phones are awesome and are very useful tools with a stupid amount of versatility. However, they are also really useful at wasting a lot of your time, but in a sneaky way. It usually won't be hours at a time. No, phones are cleverer than that. They'll just take three minutes here, seven minutes there, and thirteen minutes over here. Those minutes add up and before you know it, you've lost hours of your day to your phone.

You'll also want something to help you restrict access to all the time goblins on your phone.

Luckily, and however cliché this sounds, there's an app that.

There are hundreds. Stay Focused—App Block is a good choice for smart phones. This app allows you to have a lot more control over your phone usage along with blocking apps. You can set it to block an app after you've used it for so long or have launched an app too many times.

My personal favorite is an app called Forest–Stay Focused. This app plants a virtual tree (just like our analogy from before). The tree grows just as long as you don't leave the Forest app on your phone for whatever time you've set to focus on getting work done. If you leave early, your tree dies.

Well, that sucks.

Change between study, assignments, review, and quizzes

I studied and worked on assignments in small chunks of focused twenty-five minutes of work, followed by a five-minute break, known as the Pomodoro Technique. These twenty-five-minute time chunks help break down work into spaced intervals. Any longer and my focus and concentration would drop.

When working on something where I didn't need to keep my train of thought, I would switch up what I worked on every time I came back from a break. If I was studying/reviewing material for twenty-five minutes, I would spend the next twenty-five minutes (after breaking for five minutes) quizzing myself on what I just reviewed. After that, I would switch to working on a homework assignment.

However, I would work on the same thing for several chunks in a row if I was working on, say, a writing assignment. I liked keeping the same train of thought when writing papers. Otherwise, I wasted more time reading over what I had previously written to figure out what I should write next.

My five-minute breaks usually consisted of going for a walk outside or doing a quick set of body weight exercises to get my blood flowing. Anything to break up the sedentary lifestyle of sitting down to study or do homework for long periods of time. I used to allow myself to browse the internet or play on my phone, but those five-minute breaks would quickly turn into twenty–thirty minute breaks.

During the day, I would only socialize and goof off at lunchtime, but I had to be adamant about keeping it within my hour allotted. It's easy to convince yourself to stick around with friends and have a good time rather than to spend more time studying, but that's what your evenings and weekends are for!

In the twenty-five minutes before a class, I would review the material from the last class time. Doing that made learning and understanding the new material much easier. Right after class, I spent twenty-five minutes completing the homework for the new material while it was fresh on my mind. That combined with quizzing myself on the same material (usually just doing the homework again) the next day made it so much easier to not only make sure I was comprehending the material, but also to help me remember the material down the road.

The last hour on the job, I would pick a class and review the material from a few weeks back. That was my way of proactively studying ahead of time for an exam, which made cramming completely unnecessary.

Note: When you are going to spend time studying ahead of time, it's easy to simply read over your notes and feel like you've accomplished something. You'll read through them, feel a sense of familiarity, and feel you've accomplished something.

Wrong.

In our tree analogy, this is like walking into the woods to where you planted the tree, taking a look at it, and then walking back out of the woods. It feels like you did something, but you really didn't.

You actually need to do something with the material to help commit it to memory and reinforce it so you can recall it later. You need to quiz yourself on it. Rewrite the notes, rework homework problems, read them out loud, or explain them in your own words to someone or simply out loud to yourself. You've got to actually do something to help your tree grow; otherwise, you're just wasting your time.

The more effort you put into your review and study, the more reinforcement that information receives in long-term memory.

Don't study with crammers

The people you hang out with on a regular basis have a big influence on how you go about your college career. If you regularly hang out with crammers, you will most likely also choose that route to study.

If your closest friends are procrastinators, the odds of you becoming a procrastinator are high.

The people we spend time with have a lot of sway on how we think, talk, dress, act, etc.

I used to never curse until I started spending time in the military where a lot of the people I interacted with cursed all the time. Gradually, I started cursing more and more to the point I sounded just like them. It took a lot of effort to cut out that bad habit.

Want to lose weight? Hang out with people who eat healthily and exercise consistently. Your habits will gradually change and you'll start to eat better and get in shape.

Same goes for how you study for tests. If you hang out with people who treat college like a job, you'll most likely do the same. The opposite is most definitely true.

An easier way to determine if someone is a procrastinator is to listen and hear if they talk about how busy they are. If they constantly talk about how much work they have to get done all the time, run.

To me, busyness is a form of laziness. Yes. Laziness. That tells me you suck at time management. You have zero control or awareness of how you spend your time. Chances are you spend more time on things that you want to do versus things that need to get done. Crammers are not guarding their workday time, so they will always be "busy."

It surprises me just how talented I am at convincing

myself that I should spend time and energy on things that really don't matter. I know I need to be studying for my test that's in two weeks, but knowing that, even doing the dishes now seems more appealing and worthwhile.

There's also a weird pecking order among college students that requires bragging to determine who has the toughest school load. It goes like this:

Student 1: You wouldn't believe it, but I have two essays to write and a midterm I have to study for this week.

Student 2: Oh, you think that's something? I've got three essays, two exams, and Calculus 4 homework due tomorrow.

Student 1: Taken back by the sudden competition, they remember they also have organic chemistry homework they forgot to bring up, but before they can speak up to bolster their ranking in a pointless charade, they are stopped by the sound of laughter that gradually gets more aggressive from a third student sitting in a dark corner who overheard their debate.

Student 3: Child's play.

Student 2: Oh yeah? What'cha got?

Student 3: I've got to draft a fifty-page thesis by tonight, study for four midterms, complete eight homework assignments, and I have to prepare a ten-minute speech for my public speaking class, all while fighting off a terrible case of tuberculosis.

The first two students, knowing they have been defeated, drop to their knees and bow before the superior procrastinator. They both feel unworthy of looking them in the eye.

Sound stupid? Happens all the time. I've sadly partaken in this sad tradition. On the surface, it looks like they are simply determining who has the toughest course load. But this is merely a disguise to determine who sucks more at managing their time or who's the biggest procrastinator, though we'd like to convince ourselves otherwise.

If you continue to hang out with the crammers, you will find yourself perpetually busy and constantly in this battle of who has the worst work load.

You have to get real with yourself. Are you actually busy or are you not great at truly managing your time? Are you busy or are you good at pushing things to another day? Are you busy or are you a chronic procrastinator? Are you busy or are you just putting all of your time and effort into all the wrong priorities?

If you are like me, you need a wakeup call to stop kidding yourself.

Procrastination has bigger consequences because it doesn't stay in college once you graduate. It comes with you. We may want to believe that we can turn it on and off as we please. However, procrastination is a habit wired in our brain that comes into play whenever something that we don't feel like working on and is not due that day comes across our to-do list.

Why would you think you could do that for four straight years and it not affect you afterward? You'll have four years of experience convincing yourself that things can be completed later, anytime other than right now.

Four years is long enough to turn procrastination into a habit. Something that becomes an automatic response to a trigger. Once that trigger is set—whether or not it be assigned homework or studying ahead of time—your brain goes through a script. It asks, "Do I want to?" Nope. "Is it due today?" Nope. All signs point to pushing it off until later, so you do just that. It's what you've always done. Why would you do anything differently? Why would your behavior change after you graduate and get a job? And why would you change if those around you are procrastinating and cramming as well.

You'll have to rewire your brain to change the automatic response for pushing off assignments to tackling them early and often, especially when you don't want to. It will take work, dedication, and discipline to make it happen. And the best way to make it happen is to treat college like a full-time job and not study with crammers.

What Do You Want to Do with Your Life?

So you're treating college like a full-time job and now it's time seek some work experience in order to prepare for your first real job. Before you do, you need to know what you want to do. I love apples so freakin' much that I've considered growing my own apple trees a time or two. If you've ever looked into growing your own apple trees, you know there are a stupid amount of varieties of apples. Over 2,500 different varieties in the US alone and about 100 of those are commercially grown.

Let's say you decided to grow your own, knowing nothing about growing apples prior to the decision. You researched a little on the internet and decided to go with a particular apple because the description of what the apples looked and tasted like sounded like something you'd like.

You order your seeds and plant your trees. Over four years you've taken good care of your tree. You regularly watered it, fertilized the soil, and protected it from insects, patiently waiting to see the first apples growing from blooms. After all this time, four long years, you can now literally taste the fruits of your labor.

You pick the first ripe apple. Holding it in your hand, you realize you've been waiting for this moment for so long. You smile and bring the apple to your mouth to take that first, crisp bite. You dig your teeth into it and hear the iconic sound only biting into an apple can produce as the first burst of flavors grace your taste buds.

After a few chews, it's nothing like you expected and you find yourself spitting it out. It's not very sweet; it's tarter like a cranberry. The skin is thick and chewy and not nearly as juicy as you'd like.

Four long years, and you don't even like the apples you've grown. Had you tasted the apple or simply spoke with someone who'd tasted it before spending the time to grow the tree, you would have made a different decision.

The same thing happens when you pick a degree right outside of high school and you never actually get to taste the fruits of your labor until after you graduate.

Just like there are a hundred commercially grown apples, you can choose from over a hundred majors. You might have picked a major strictly from reading a short description of what people with that major do during career day at your high school. Or people said you were good at math, science, or art, so you decided to go with your perceived strength by majoring in accounting, engineering, or graphic design respectively.

Four years go by and you find yourself landing a job in your major, but you quickly realize you don't care for that particular line of work.

Had you experienced different jobs in your major, or at least spoken to someone currently holding your desired job, you would have a better idea of what you actually want to do, and more importantly, what you don't want to do.

Internships let you taste different jobs in your major before ever graduating, which is another great reason to pursue getting an internship as early on in your college career as you can.

You want to taste your apple sooner rather than later. As soon as you can start applying for internships, do it. Get your foot in the door to get experience in an area of your career field to help you determine what route you want to take (and what route you want to steer clear of).

I don't care if your GPA isn't stellar, whether you're a freshmen, or if your school doesn't have a career center to help you find an internship. You should be searching for and applying for internships every semester.

Go ahead and ask yourself some questions that will also help narrow down your options:

-What classes did you enjoy the most?

-What classes did you enjoy the least?

-Do you want to work close to home? Far away? Internationally? Don't care?

-Do you want to work in an office or be out and about?

-Do you want a job that travels a lot?

Answering these simple questions helps again to narrow down your choices. Once you have it narrowed to three choices, do more research on jobs that fit those three choices and find out everything you can about them.

If you are flying by the seat of your pants and have no idea what you want to do, then hold onto your underwear. You've got work to do.

LinkedIn.com, a professional social media site, allows you to find people currently in the jobs you're interested in. Shoot them a message like this on the platform:

Hello [insert name], I'm a year out from graduating with a degree in [insert blank], and I saw you hold a position as a/the [insert job]. I was wondering if you had some time to chat with me about a-day-in-the-life as a [insert job]. Thank you for your consideration.

Not everyone will respond to your message. The majority might very well ignore it. That's fine. You only need one, though it's better to have more. It's great to talk to multiple people who hold the same position because they will all have different experiences and opinions based on whether they like their job.

If you use the LinkedIn route, make sure you polish up your profile (or make one if you haven't already) and have a professional photo as your profile picture and not the photo of you at the toga party from Facebook.

Speaking of profiles, go through your other social media accounts and see if you have anything on them that may make someone second guess wanting to hire you. View your profile from the perspective of a hiring manager. You may have forgotten about a few distasteful posts or pictures you're tagged in. If you've got a lot of questionable photos and posts, it might be advantageous to just completely delete your account and make a new one. Sounds a little overkill, but if your chances of employment are at stake, it's worth it.

You'll need to take some time to understand your options. Research all you can do with your potential degree choices. You can either stop by the career services center on campus or do a simple web search to see all the different jobs you can get with a particular degree. The results can be plentiful or not so much, depending on what you major in. Use this research to narrow down what you think you want to do. After that, forget about all your other options . . . for now at least.

This research serves a lot of different purposes. For one, it helps you to determine not only what you think you might want to do, but what you don't want to do, which is just as important.

Get intimate with the day-in-the-life of people holding

those jobs. Talk to professors to see what they know about those jobs. See if they know someone who is working or has worked in that position and see if the professor would be willing to connect you both to chat.

Hopefully, after doing all that research, talking to professors, and creepily stocking people of LinkedIn, you ultimately find out that one of your three options is something you'd like to pursue.

If not, turn back to all your other options and try again. Hopefully, you started a year out so you have plenty of time to figure out what path you want to take.

If your research was fruitful, meaning one, two, or all three of your options are something you'd like to pursue, now you can and should work toward landing a job or an internship in those positions.

Seek Work Experience

It's fantastic how accessible higher education has become for so many people in the US. As amazing as that is, it has created a new problem for those seeking employment after graduating. Because accessibility has risen over the years, the value of having an associates'/bachelor's degree has dropped significantly.

I mentioned earlier that 43 percent of college graduates with a four-year degree are underemployed, meaning that almost half of those that graduate with a degree are in a job that doesn't even require a degree.

That's insane!

It's like a coin toss as to whether you will actually get a job you went to college for in the first place.

Why spend all that time and energy and money getting a degree to end up with a job that doesn't even require it?

And I'm positive that you would rather not be underemployed and underpaid, right?

You'd probably like to know how you can be a part of the 57 percent who actually get a job after graduating that requires a four-year degree, wouldn't you?

First, you need to realize that just going to college does not guarantee you will get a job that requires a degree. At some point in history that was the case.

Now, everyone and their mother has a degree. The value of having a degree has gone down now that the workforce has been saturated with people with four-year degrees and with not enough four-year degree level jobs to go around.

These non-degree jobs certainly don't pay as much as their four-year degree counterparts.

Of course, you might think that you'll eventually get a job that requires a degree and the first job doesn't matter that much in the long run.

Unfortunately, so many students approach employment this way. You can see it on their faces at college career fairs the semester they are to graduate. They run around booth to booth, waiting in line behind other students just to hand out their resume to whatever company will take it, hoping someone will call them in for an interview.

Their resume will be in a stack of hundreds of other resumes, and unless something on it makes them stand out among their peers, it will just look like every other resume.

They'll wait months for a reply, and for a while, they'll continue pushing out their resume on websites advertising jobs in their field, but once again, they're competing with hundreds (if not thousands) of other people submitting their resume for the exact same jobs.

Eventually, their student loan debt's grace period will end, and the notices will pile in their mailbox letting them know payments are due soon. They'll start feeling the pressure to get a job. Any job. Something to start bringing a paycheck in to start chipping away at the mountain of student loan debt.

Next thing they know they accept a job they are overqualified for and that underpays them.

But there's still hope, right? Just because the first job isn't exactly what they were gunning for doesn't mean they won't eventually get the job they're qualified for.

I wish that were the case.

Unfortunately, the report also stated that those who are initially underemployed are five times more likely to still be underemployed after five years, and it gets progressively harder to escape the underemployed trap the longer you stay in it.

This all boils down to one thing: the first job straight out of college is critical.

The degree itself used to stand as a differentiator among your peers. Now that so many of your peers also have a degree, you now need something else to set you apart from everyone else. Employees now seek new graduates who have work experience in their field.

This creates a chicken before the egg scenario.

You got a degree so you could get the job, but to get the job, you need work experience, which would require you to have a job to begin with.

Wait, what?

Trust me; the frustration is mutual.

You might be thinking, Well then how do I gather the work experience to land the job?

You get it before you even graduate, that's how. You either get an internship or a co-op position as a student to work in whatever industry you're gunning for.

For example, say you're an accounting major looking to grab some work experience before graduating to up your chances of getting the job you want (or a job at all) when you graduate.

You manage to grab an internship with a local accounting firm over the summer before your junior year. You work closely with accountants and a couple of CPAs who teach you the ins and outs of running a firm: how they attract and treat clients, how to run audits; how to do taxes; and how to manage bookkeeping. They even pay you above minimum wage, which will help pay for school. Sure, you might be making coffee and running errands, but the experience you'll gain from actually putting your education to work is priceless.

The next summer, you then leverage your experience with the accounting firm to snag another internship with a large hospital for their billing and accounting department. You gain even more experience doing that all the while figuring out what specific accounting work you'd like to apply for.

By the time you graduate, you'll have two summers' worth of experience in two different niches of accounting. You're now a competitive applicant for open jobs you're interested in. Plus, you're not too worried about landing a job because both the hospital and the accounting firm offered you jobs upon graduating because of the great work you did while interning with them.

What's the difference between a co-op and an internship?

A co-op is typically more than one semester and separated by semesters of school. For example, my first co-op semester was over the summer. The next fall, I was back in school followed by another co-op semester in the spring, school over the summer, and my last co-op semester in the fall. School and work alternated semesters, though this is not always the case.

An internship is typically for only one semester usually during the summer. These can be paid or unpaid. A lot of my friends strictly did internships over the summer so they didn't have to delay graduation. Certainly not a bad choice. Some internships can have flexible schedules where you actually work on days you are not in class.

Since I've done both a co-op and internship, if I could go back, I would have done strictly internships to experience several different industries, companies, and challenges along the way. You get a large breadth of different paths in your career choice versus a co-op which gives you more depth in a specific niche in your career choice.

How to get internships/co-op jobs

You can take several different approaches to landing internships and co-op jobs while in school. Some colleges and universities offer programs to find internships for their students. Mississippi State University, for example, invites companies out to their career fair to meet students who are looking for work experience. Students can even sign up for interviews with companies to land an internship or co-op position or full-time job.

If your school doesn't have such a program, you'll just have to be more proactive to find internships around you. You can take several different paths. You can start calling local businesses, you can walk into local businesses, you can apply online, and you can reach out to your network.

Let's assume our accountant student's college doesn't have a robust career center.

To find his own, he called and walked into local accounting firms in the area. He asked if he could apply for an internship. Some said they didn't offer such a position, some had never heard of such a thing, and others never got back to him. After being persistent, one firm gladly hired him for the summer in exchange for cheaper labor and performing a tedious and routine task around the office.

You might have to do very much the same. You might have to talk to quite a few different businesses or companies to land an internship that relates to your degree. For some, they might never have had or thought about having an intern; however, they might be open to the idea. Sell yourself as someone truly interested in gaining experience in the field.

They might not be able to pay you. That's okay. Ultimately, you want experience before you graduate; however, you will have to decide whether working for free is worth it.

My personal favorite is reaching out to your network. Your chances of getting an internship are much higher if you have someone on the inside vouching for you compared to cold calling or submitting a resume.

Talk with your parents, close family, or family friends to see if they know anyone who works somewhere that offers such a program/position. Tell them you are looking for an internship in whatever major you're in, during a certain time period (e.g., over the summer), and hopefully paid but willing to work for experience. Some of them might know some people, some of them might be the people you need to talk to, and others might not know anyone all, but you won't know until you start asking.

If they do know someone, they might introduce you to them, they may reach out to them on your behalf, and others might have you reach out to them and simply have you tell them that so-and-so said you should contact them.

Let's say you are looking for a mechanical engineer internship in your area. You happen to live near a large concrete factory that hires engineers. Your neighbor just so happens to work there, so you approach him and tell him you're in the market for an engineering internship and wondering if the company does such a thing.

He goes to work the next week and asks around and finds out the engineering department does. In fact, they have two positions for internships, and one is currently vacant for the following summer. He puts in a good word for you and manages to set up an on-site interview, which you totally rock and land the job for the summer.

After speaking with family and friends, talk with your professors to see if they know anyone who might offer what you are looking for. Just because they are in academia, doesn't mean they haven't done work in their field. Even if they've always been a professor, they still might know someone in the field. A lot of professors perform research for companies, military, and the government at the local, state, or federal level. Their network could be beefy, even though they've been lecturing and/or conducting research their entire career.

They might even know people who they went to school with who went into the private sector upon graduating.

It pays to be on good terms with that professor before approaching them with your request. If you hardly show up to class, hardly participate, and your grades are poor, you better believe they'll think twice before reaching out to their network for you. Just another reason to be an above average student.

Lastly, shoot out a message to your social media network. Start with linkedin.com since that platform is built for such a request. Then try Facebook. Your message should be short and to the point.

"I'm looking for an [insert major] internship for the summer of [year] to gain experience and insight in my career field. I'm not above making coffee and running errands."

Afterward, apply online for internships in your career field (i.e. www.indeed.com). Be sure to check out the resume section coming up in the book on how to smash your resume before submitting one.

When you've exhausted all online applications, start contacting local companies for internships, whether by phone or in person or email. Either route, your introduction is the same. Mention you're a student at so-and-so college/university and looking for an internship in [insert field] to gain experience and insight while putting your education to work.

No matter which way you go about finding a co-op or internship, your first move is to research the company before you ever show up to an interview or call someone on the phone. You should do this regardless if you are applying for an internship or a full-time job.

Find out what the company does, find out their history, try and find out where they are going, major changes in the company or industry, questions you want to ask, etc. Find out anything and everything about them that you can.

Depending on whether the company is public, meaning anyone can go buy stock and become a shareholder of that company, you might be able to get your hands on the annual report from the CEO to the shareholders.

This report contains a lot of financial reports (cash flow, reported earning, and other boring stuff). You can skip all that and read the sections on the company's strategy, challenges, and opportunities over the past year and what to expect the following year.

This is a gold mine of info you can use to draft questions to ask during an interview.

You can find the annual report by doing a web search of the "[company name] + annual report + [year]."

If you can't get your hands on an annual report, no worries. You'll just have to do some more digging on the internet. Start with their website and find out as much as you can about them.

Most companies also have social media accounts you can follow. The more you know about their history, where they've been, where they are now, and where they want to go, the better your questions will be that will lead to great discussions during the interview.

It's these discussions that will help your interviewer remember who you are. They might be doing twenty interviews over a short period of time for the same position and it's hard to remember how each candidate performed.

The last thing you can do is simply talk to the people who work at the company you want to work for. What better way to learn more about a company than by talking with the people that actually work there. If you don't know anyone who works there, you can use a website called LinkedIn.com to find them. We'll talk more about this in a bit.

This will certainly take some work up front, but it will surely pay off in the long run. This information you're gathering will be incorporated into your summary statement on your resume and questions you ask during the interview and practice for when you eventually graduate and apply for full-time jobs.

Then let fate/destiny take over. There is a good chance you'll get a lot of noes or no responses. No worries, you just need one yes. Just one!

How I got my first co-ops job

I searched for co-ops and internships the day my parents dropped me off for college.

After putting away my few belongings in my 175 sq. ft. dorm, it was time for my parents to say goodbye. My mom teared up, gave me a hug, told me how proud she was, and got into their car to leave. My dad then shook my hand and looked me in the eye. I had waited for this moment for a long time. The moment my father would see me as worthy of his praise and say, "You are a man now. I am very proud to be your father. You bring much honor to your family." As he spoke, maybe even a small tear would grow out of the corner of his eye. It would never fall, but it would be noticeable.

Instead, my father smirked as he said, "I have six kids. I cannot help you. Good luck." He then got in the car and left.

What he meant was "I am completely and utterly

broke. If at any point you expected financial support from your family, you are wrong. Completely and utterly wrong. You are not allowed to move back in. See you at Thanksgiving. Good luck."

Sadly, I had not even thought about my financial situation up until this point. After they left, I checked my student account to ease my nerves, but it had the opposite effect. I had already accrued several thousand dollars in tuition, housing costs, obscurely labeled fees, and a meal plan.

How the heck was I supposed to pay for all this? Student loans were always an option, but I was completely against them. So I did what any rational human being would do and suppressed the thought of my financial ruin deep into the back of my subconscious and lived in blissful denial.

It wasn't until halfway through the semester that I found a solution to my dilemma. A student came into our Introduction to Electrical Engineering class and gave a presentation about his internship experience. I couldn't have cared less and only heard . . .

Blah Blah Blah

Work Experience

Blah

Great Opportunity

Blah

Resume

Blah

Twenty-five dollars per hour

That last part I heard clearly, and I immediately blurted out, "Where can I sign up?" That student directed me to the campus career center where they gave me the lowdown on the whole program but warned me that they rarely hire freshman or sophomores. Rarely to me meant there was still a micro-ounce of hope to cling to.

Even with their warning, I scheduled two interviews:

one with a power plant back near my hometown and the other with a steel plant in north Alabama close to where my grandparents lived.

I hadn't done many interviews prior to these. Just a handful that were for minimum wage jobs. Nothing to this scale. I did a ton of research on both companies and did whatever I could to show I was worth their time and investment. As a first-semester freshman without a GPA yet, I really didn't have much to offer.

Long story short, I gave those interviews everything I had. Ultimately, I got both job offers and ended up taking the co-op job with the steel plant, which guaranteed three full semesters of work. Those three semesters gave me not only enough money to pay for school, but they also let me acquire a full year's worth of engineering experience.

That experience helped me land another internship at a fertilizer plant for additional experience and more cash for school.

Though I originally co-opted and interned for the

money, the experience was incredible. I actually got to use what I was learning in class in a practical way. Secondly, since I was so young, a lot of what I was learning on the job were concepts I normally wouldn't have seen until junior and senior year. This gave me a leg up on my peers during those classes.

Most importantly, I realized I didn't want to do engineering work inside a plant or factory environment. Learning that ahead of time helped me narrow down what I really wanted to do with my degree.

In the end, knowing I didn't like industry work, I joined the Air Force as an officer and used my degree for the warfighter.

Sure, it took me five years to graduate instead of four thanks to my co-op/internship, but it was well worth it. Walking out of college debt free and with a job before graduating is a complete game changer when starting any career.

Resumes

Resumes are funny things. Your resume is like a little representative that informs potential employers about how freakin' cool you are. However, just because you have one, it doesn't mean it will do a great job. It must be well informed of your experience, knowledge, skills, and achievements along with knowing how to craft that information to match the specific position you are applying for. If you don't spend much time working with your representative, your representation will most likely do a horrible job doing the only thing it's supposed to do: market you. It may look easy but putting together a well-crafted resume takes time and effort and a touch a personalization for each individual company you will send your representative to.

The last thing you want to do is put a bunch of time into teaching your representative everything about you but not put enough emphasis on making sure your representative knows a thing or two about correct spelling, punctuation, grammar, etc. It might know and say everything your potential employer wants to hear, but a representative with typos will not communicate well and wonky formatting will have an unprofessional appearance. Your rep will be kicked into a trashcan Spartan style.

In order to ensure it's ready to represent you well, you should send your representative to others for a trial run. You might like the fact your rep goes on and on about your middle school accomplishments so you will need someone else to let you know that no one cares and that space is better used for something else.

I know, I thought all those gold star stickers stood for something too.

To make sure your representative is in tip-top shape, you want to make a master resume before you craft individual ones. This master resume should have all your past work experience, community service, degrees, awards, skills, and references that will help uniquely sell you. Everything. Every little thing should find its way onto your master resume. Don't worry about how it's formatted, how many pages, or anything like that. This is just to have everything in a central place.

You're going to pull information from that master resume to craft individual resumes for the specific positions or jobs you want to apply for. Not everything will make the cut.

Formatting

There are a ca-trillion different ways to format your resume, so I'm not going to advise you to pick a specific one. My only suggestion is to keep it simple.

The resume that I used had a very complex and fully customized formatting built by yours truly. It looked great in the end, but man was it a pain to edit. One simple adjustment would send everything out of whack. I spent more time formatting the information than on the information itself. Do yourself a favor and keep it as simple as possible.

I recommend just using an online resource that will do all the formatting for you like:

https://www.myperfectresume.com/

https://zety.com/

You just need to plug in your information from your master resume and the site does all the heavy lifting for you. These sites can help you get three pages' worth of information into one.

Whether or not you make your own or use an online resource, send it off to a few people for edits and comments after you have made a decent attempt at crafting it. If anything, take it to your career services center on campus to review it.

If you are tailoring your resume for a specific job in your career field, I like to send the job description with my resume so anyone reviewing my resume will have a better idea as to what I'm tailoring it for.

Everyone is going to have their own opinion of how it should look, but mainly you're looking for feedback on how your resume makes you sound and look as a potential candidate for a job and if anything glaring needs to be removed, like using unicorns as bullets for bullet statements or stuff like that.

After getting their comments back and making any needed edits, ask some of your professors or any of your connections who are currently holding the job you want to review your resume. Be sure to ask if they even want to look over it before you send it over to them. If they are willing to take a look, shoot it off to them pronto. If possible, ask them in person and have a copy ready if they agree to look over it.

If you want to, send a thank you email or card thanking them for their time. They just did you a solid so at least take the extra step and thank them for it.

Job specific resumes

Just like I mentioned earlier when I said there are a ca-trillion different ways to format a resume, there are also a ca-trillion different way to word your resume to match the job you are applying for. You'll find websites, books, YouTube videos and who knows what else just talking about what you should do with your resume so you can stand out and get called in for an interview.

One of the most common advice you'll get is match your work experience and skill set to what the job position is looking for.

In the end, you want to look like the perfect candidate for the job. On paper at least.

A lot of people use the same resume for each job they are applying for. The last thing you want to do is shotgun out the same resume to every job post online that's of interest to you. This is almost as useful as printing out a bunch of copies of your resume and throwing them out the window as you drive down the highway.

You'll want to customize your resume for each individual position.

You might be thinking, By golly, that sounds like it would take a lot of time to do that for each job.

You are correct; it does take a lot of time. You want to know what also takes a lot of time? Landing an interview from an employer desperate enough to take a chance on someone who sends out generic resumes.

Think of it this way, every time you submit a customized resume, you're cutting out most of the competition who didn't.

Let's say the job description states they are looking for someone that has experience in project management in IT systems. You would then want to have something on your resume that at least shows that you have experience in either project management or IT systems, and preferably both.

But this is easier said than done. It can be kind of difficult to match your resume perfectly with what the employer is looking for, especially if you don't have a lot of experience in your career field, considering you are a college student or a recent graduate.

In those cases, I like to have a section on my resume of skills I'm currently acquiring. This is a section that I can modify easily for particular jobs that require a certain skill set.

When you look for jobs online, you'll see a section on the job posting about knowledge, skills, and abilities which is where the employer will list out what they are looking for in a candidate for the position.

Let's say you are applying for a business analyst position. On the job description underneath the knowledge, skill, and abilities section, you see the following:

- Proficient using Microsoft Office Suite
- Ability to interpret financial reports
- Ability to respond to inquiries or complaints

from customers

- Ability to present information to top management
- General knowledge of SQL databases

Reading through them you might feel confident you meet most of what's listed. You've used Microsoft office since grade school, you took an entire class on reading and interpreting financial reports to do stock investing evaluations, and you are very confident in your ability to present material and speak in public. All these things you'd have no problem presenting in some fashion on your resume.

But that last one about SQL . . . well, you don't have the slightest clue as to what that is. That's where your "skills I'm currently acquiring" section comes in. You can list SQL as one of them. This allows you to put SQL on your resume without having prior experience.

But do you just list it there and not actually go look into what SQL is? Of course not. You'll want to go out and start researching what this is all about, but you don't have to spend a lot of time looking for it.

In three minutes, I found out what SQL is, a standard programming language for access and manipulating data in a database, I found YouTube videos that would explain the fundamentals of how SQL works, and I even found a website that offered a free course on SQL.

In a few hours of going through the material, I found I could have a decent understanding of SQL concepts and maybe even know how to start using the programming language to access and manipulate data in databases.

Is it worth the effort?

Absolutely.

The person in charge of going through all the resumes they receive is not going to take the time to thoroughly read through everything you put on yours. The first thing they will do is find reasons to throw yours in the trash to significantly cut down the amount that will be considered for an interview.

One of those disqualifiers they may look for is a mention of SQL. They will skim your resume and if they don't find anything on it about SQL, that's a perfectly good reason to not even consider you for an interview.

Career fairs

Most colleges and universities will host career fairs on their campuses for companies looking to hire recent graduates or students looking for internships.

In these cases, you may not be able to customize your resume for each individual position. In this case, you'll use your generic resume that's tailored to your specific career field versus tailored toward a specific job position in your career field.

However, that doesn't mean you can't do some straight up ninja techniques to tailor *some* of your resumes.

If you know some of the companies that will be there, you can make a few resumes specifically for these companies you're really interested in. You will stand out like a sore thumb but in a good way. I guarantee you 99 percent of students would not think to do this.

The easiest way to modify your resume for a specific company who is attending the career fair is to have a purpose statement. This is an optional section on a resume and typically goes below the header where you name, email, phone number, etc. goes.

The summary sells your unique marketable skills and will be the first thing employers see when they look at your resume.

Most candidates put something like this:

Looking for an [insert job] role where I can apply my skills and abilities to make a difference.

Well . . . it doesn't get more vanilla than that.

Instead, you want to use the summary statement to

highlight your skills, what job you want, what company you want to work for, and how you can add value to the company.

You can use a template that you just fill in like this:

[**desirable trait**]+[**major**]+[**graduate/student**] looking to fill a position as a [**job position**] at [**company name**]. Seeking to leverage [**skill 1**] and [**skill 2**] to help [**company name**] with your upcoming goals and challenges.

Note: it's better to write this after your resume is complete so you can pull your skills from your current job experience.

An accountant student who has data analysis and auditing experience from prior internships might write:

Highly motivated accounting student looking to fill a position as an accounting intern at the Hawthorne CPA Firm. Seeking to leverage data analysis and auditing skills to help Hawthorne CPA Firm with your upcoming goals and challenges.

To better tailor that last sentence toward the specific company, actually list their goals and challenges found in their company's mission or vision statement.

It's that simple, and you don't have to follow this format to a T. This is just a guide. Make sure to switch out the company name and position for each individual resume.

Just make sure you don't hand out the wrong resume to the wrong company. Nothing would be more off-putting than handing a resume meant for Coca-Cola when it was meant to go to Pepsi.

For all the other companies you are not as excited about but would be willing to work for or intern with or ones you didn't know would be there, you can have your generic resume ready to go.

Paper

While you could print your resume on plain white paper (just like everyone else), I recommended using a different type of paper. You could use official resume paper from an office supply store or cardstock. Cardstock is heavier and feels more official.

I like to print my resume on ivory paper, which you can also get at office supply stores. It just looks so freakin' legit that your resume will stand out.

My friend suggested I do this, and I thought it was stupid. It was like twelve dollars for just twenty-five sheets of ivory paper, but he was a smart guy, so I listened to him.

When I passed out my resume at the career fair, every single prospective employer commented on my resume paper. That alone got me an in to start up a conversation with the employees who were assigned to recruit at the job fair.

At one booth, six other students were handing in resumes and the recruiter grabbed mine and said, "Wow! That is a nice resume. This looks great!" The other students were not happy with me showing them up, but this is not a playground. Every single one of us is trying to get a job and why wouldn't you do whatever you can to stand out? Best twelve dollars I've ever spent.

Interviews

Interviews can be stressful. As they should be. You've been working for the past four years (or more!) for this moment. To represent the last several years of hard work. To convince someone that you deserve a chance at full-time employment.

These interviews can be over the phone, over a Skype call, or face-to-face. All of these have their pros and cons that you should be aware of. It's not uncommon to deal with all three for the same job.

But no matter what type of interview it is, you'll want to practice before experiencing the real thing.

Mock interviews

Basic training in the military is stressful and chaotic before you even get off the bus to start. Wide-eyed high schoolers with clinched butt cheeks quickly realize the world they just volunteered for offers little sleep, peace of mind, and suck sandwiches for breakfast, lunch, and dinner. Large and intimidating instructors are like sharks and can smell the slightest whiff of weakness, which will be immediately addressed with yelling, knife hands, questions with no existing correct answer, and push-ups.

These future soldiers are broken down and built back up with constant and consistent training that requires excellence under intense pressure.

From the outside, this treatment looks cruel and inhumane, but the opposite is true. This stress and chaos is for each trainees' better good, instilling in them the confidence and awareness to operate efficiently under the stress and chaos of war. This increases their chances of survival and success to complete the mission so when they taste the first bite of the suck sandwich on the front line, it's not the first time.

Interviews should be treated the same.

It's hard to believe that any student would work for years to get a degree with the ultimate goal of landing a full-time job and not practice the single most important aspect of landing a job: the interview. Sadly it happens all the time. Several of my peers waltzed into interviews for jobs their senior year without ever practicing what it's like to be in an interview. Unless you count that interview in high school for the part-time job at Arby's, they walked into a high-stakes environment with no experience.

They weren't getting the job.

They'd walk out of the interview dejected feeling like the whole interview was a train wreck. The crazy part was they wouldn't have one earthly idea as to why it went so bad.

If the first time you are exposed to the stresses of being interviewed for a job is the real deal, don't be surprised when you don't get it. With so much at stake, you need a handful of dry runs to prepare you for when it counts, whether or not it's for an internship or a full-time job.

To do this effectively, mock interviews are the way to go. The more you expose yourself to that environment, the more comfortable you'll be. Just like soldiers who are fully capable of performing under pressure, the more experience you have being interviewed, the more confident and well put together you'll appear, and the more likely you'll get the job.

- That's what makes mock interviews so important. You can go about them in several different ways: check to see if your school offers mock interviews through the career center

- Set up your own mock interviews with fellow students

- Have a mock interview with one of your willing professors

- Have an interview with one of your new connections you've made when you searched for people who have the jobs you want

For any of those options, you've got to simply ask to make it happen. Doing a combination of each is not a bad idea. Remember, the more exposure you get, the better you will be at handling the pressure during the real interview.

Participate in roughly five mock interviews, mixing face-to-face, phone, and Skype interviews because all of those could be the chosen interview style of your prospective employer.

My only interview for my second internship was strictly over the phone. There was no face-to-face interview following that one. Had I not practiced giving phone interviews prior, I doubt I would have done well during my interview.

Either way, take all of your mock interviews seriously. Prepare, dress the part, and treat them like the real thing.

Several mock interview will also help expose you to the different types of questions that typically get asked during interviews. You'll notice a lot of the questions won't be focused on your particular major and how much you paid attention in class. Instead, they will be more focused on finding out who you are as a person.

If you know some upper classmen in your major who have already gone through interviews for internships or for full-time jobs, ask them how their interviews went and what questions they were asked. This will give you a better idea of what to expect and how to prepare for your interview.

You'll hear questions about:

- Your community involvement
- How you handle conflict
- How you manage your time
- How you deal with stress
- What leadership experience you have
- What hobbies or interest you have
- Where you see yourself in five years

- A time you had to make a tough decision
- Etc.

Each question will require you to reach back into your past experiences to pull examples. This is where a story bank comes in handy.

Prepare a story bank

A story bank is simply a list of your past experiences related to a topic. If the topic is conflict, for example, you'll want to create a list of all the times you dealt with a conflict and how you resolved it. Not all the stories you write down will be noteworthy, but a few of them will be very useful for when you get asked a question about dealing with conflict. These stories should show you dealing with conflict in a professional manner.

If you are having a hard time thinking of stories, ask your family or friends if they can think of anything involving you and the topic.

The more mock interviews you do, the more practice you'll have recalling and telling these stories to answer questions, and the more natural and relaxed you'll sound during a real interview.

Pros and cons of phone and online interviews.

Phone interviews

Phone interviews are a very common interview option, especially for interviews that have multiple rounds. Phone interviews are typically the first round before moving on to the next round, which will either be a Skype or face-to-face interview.

Phone interviews are great because they can be done practically anywhere you have a phone connection.

You can conduct the phone interview in traffic, eating a burrito, or in a banana costume. Should you, though? Probably not.

You should find a quiet place to have the phone interview and make sure it's somewhere with a good connection. And even though they can't see you, you should dress the part. This will make you feel more professional; thus, you will act more professional. And save that burrito for a celebratory feast after you crush the phone interview.

Another pro of phone interview is you can have a copy of your resume for reference, a list of questions you don't want to forget to ask, and answers to typical interview questions right in front of you. Just don't read from them like a script. You will sound unauthentic. I also recommend having something to write with and write on to take notes.

Some cons of the phone interview are having no reference of facial expressions, body language, or anything like that. All you know is the tone of their voice. You miss out on the non-verbal communication that helps you determine if what you are saying is what they are looking for. You can't see head nods, eyebrow raises, frowns, or someone leaning over slightly to release gas without you noticing. All that information is golden, but you get none of it. You're out in the middle of the phone interview wilderness without a compass.

They also can't see your non-verbals, and without people in front of you, you might not sound engaging. To compensate, stand up during the interview. This will help you sounds more energetic. Also, smile during the interview when you speak. This will literally change your tone into something more pleasant and cheerful to hear on the other end.

Online interviews

I personally hate online interviews. So many things can go wrong during one. The audio could be spotty, the video could freeze up, or you could experience that weird thing where the audio comes through five seconds before the video catches up. Technology has certainly gotten better over the years but it's still not great for conducting an interview.

With that in mind, here are some things you can do to help make sure the process goes as smoothly as possible.

- Find a place with a reliable Wi-Fi connection. After you've found your location, whether or not it's at home, a university, or library, test out whatever software your interviewer is going to use, Skype, Zoom, etc. Host a few test meetings with people you know to see how reliable your connection is and to just make sure your audio and video work.
- Use headphones with an audio input to help with the sound quality.
- Dress professionally like you would for a face-to-face interview.

- Make sure there is nothing questionable in the background behind you.

- Have a Plan B. If during the interview you notice the connection isn't great, suggest switching to a phone interview.

Interview tips

Regardless of which interview style it is, you need to follow standard rules:

<u>1) Never pull answers out of your butt</u>

You will feel the nagging pressure to answer every question asked with some profound statement to show how intelligent, overqualified, and perfect you are for the job. You might think that if you don't have an answer to a question immediately, the interviewer thinks you are an idiot and unworthy. To ensure that doesn't ever happen, it may feel perfectly acceptable to pull answers out of thin air and just make something up hoping pure, golden Shakespeare pores out of your mouth.

Just don't.

It's perfectly acceptable to say, "I don't know."

Is it ideal? No, but it's more respectable to be honest and know your limitations than for the interviewer's BS radar to fire off while you are obviously trying to hide the fact you have no idea what you are talking about.

When I interviewed for a paid co-op position my freshman year, I answered with "I don't know" to the majority of the questions concerning my major. As a first-semester freshman, I hadn't even began to touch any of the core classes of my major. I didn't know the first thing about electrical engineering.

I wasn't sure about half the questions they asked, but I was sure I wasn't going to get the job.

To my surprise, I received a call over Christmas break

with a job offer. I about dropped the phone. A few weeks into the job, I wondered why I was even offered the job to begin with. There were plenty of qualified upperclassmen from several different schools that applied and were interviewed. Why did they pick the guy who knew nothing at all? So I asked them, and their answer surprised me.

"One reason was because you were honest," they said.

Come to find out, one of the reasons why I thought I wouldn't get the job (being an idiot when it came to my major and being honest about it) was actually a reason I got it in the first place.

So be honest, and don't pull answers out of your butt.

2) What's your kryptonite?

A question about your greatest weakness is not a time to twist a weakness into a strength.

I can't tell you how many people I've heard answer this

question that goes like this:

"I just work way too many hours."

"I simply don't know when to give up."

"I'm just too freakin' good looking."

That's not what they are looking for. They want to know you have the situational awareness to recognize your own faults and, more importantly, you're doing something about it. I brought up two true faults during my interviews:

1.   I tend to prioritize menial tasks when I should be doing a more important task that either seems difficult or I'm not sure how to start or finish. I've started to recognize when I'm avoiding priorities and reading the book *The One Thing* by Gary Keller has helped me tremendously.

•

2.   I love to talk. I love chitchat. As great as that is for getting to know the people I work with, I know firsthand, I sometimes cross that fine line where

chitchat becomes a distraction for not only myself, but for others as well. My approach for dealing with this is using time blocking. I schedule time for chitchat during the early mornings, during lunch, and after office hours to ensure I'm getting work completed.

You are going to want to identify your weaknesses and present these with a solution to combat them. Do not make up your weaknesses. Be honest.

3) Questions

In the start, the interviewer will be asking you the questions. But near the end, the floor will be handed over to you.

The interviewer will ask, "Do you have any questions for me?" and now the tables have turned. Now you get to be the interviewer.

Do not show up without having several questions of your own to ask at the end of your interview.

This is where you'll make back some bonus points for being honest about not knowing an answer to a question or not having stellar answers for every question you get asked. All that research you did will come in handy here.

You can ask questions like:

- How would you describe the culture?
- How are employees incentivized?
- Does the company tend to hire within or from outside the organization?

But these questions are very generic in nature. You can certainly ask these types of questions, but you'll want to ask questions that are specific to the company you are applying for, which comes from doing research and really getting to know the company you want to work for.

When I was interviewed for a co-op position at a steel plant, I did a ton of research on the company about their history, issues they were facing, and anything new they were trying out.

- I asked them why they first built mini steel mills in rural areas surrounded by farmland instead of near large cities where it would be easier to find employees.

- I asked them about some of the by-products that were created through the steel production process. One by-product was a fine metallic dust that had been collected and stored on-site. I asked if they were planning on recycling it or had plans to sell it in any way.

Both those questions led to great discussions, helped show I did my research, and proved I was more than interested in working for the company as an intern.

For my internship interviews, I'd ask specific questions about previous interns if there was time left. I'd ask about what projects they worked on, what expectations were set for them, and anything else that came to mind.

4) Business cards

Something you can easily do after the interview is request their business card if they have one. By doing this, you have their email address, so you can shoot them a message within forty-eight hours simply thanking them for their time and consideration.

This helps them to remember who you were and stand out from everyone else who didn't shoot them a message to ups your chances of being a top candidate for the job.

Conclusion

Goodness gracious have we've covered some ground or what? First off, kudos on you for actually finishing the book. Sure, it's not a long one, but you managed to pull through and that's worth a pat on the back.

Secondly, I hope I've opened your eyes to the possibilities that are available to you while in college if you're willing to put in the effort.

Even if you only implement 10 percent of what this book covers, you'll suck 10 percent less.

Neat.

Keep it handy and refer back to it as you need it.

I wish you the best of luck on your journey, and in your career.

fist bump

-Cody

Do **<u>NOT</u>** leave the book before grabbing a copy of my collection of 127+ FREE online resources for college students. . .

you will regret it!

http://rebrand.ly/collegeresources

Again, as a thank you for getting a copy of the book, I want to share with you my collection of 127+ college resources.

With it your friends will wonder:

- How you get your assignments done so quickly?
- Why you seem so confident going into interviews?
- How you stay effortlessly organized?
- Why your resume looks like a professional team put it together?
- How you study less yet make better grades?
- And so much more!

The best part? I'm continuously added to it when I come across great resources that need to be added to the list.

>> Go here: http://rebrand.ly/collegeresources to get instant access to my list of 127+ college resources!

ABOUT CODY SMITH

Cody Smith graduated Magna Cum Laude from Mississippi State University with a Bachelor of Science in electrical engineering. He graduated 100 percent free of student loan debt thanks to landing a paid co-op his freshman year. During his time in college, he learned the best way to treat college is like a full-time job.

He writes books on crowdfunding, public speaking, and college, went LARPing once (never again), and has applied for Pirate School.

They have not got back to him . . .

Cody currently lives in Mississippi and is crushing several new writing projects waiting to be published.

You can connect with Cody via email:

cody@fearpunchingcody.com

NEED SOME HELP?

Could you use some help preparing for interviews, researching a company, resumes, or receiving some general guidance with this whole college thing?

I'd love to offer my services to help you.

It's not free, but there is a student discount *wink*

Simply shoot me a message at:

cody@fearpunchingcody.com

REQUEST FOR A REVIEW

What did you think about *Your Best College Guide*?

First and foremost, thank you for purchasing *Your Best College Guide* and making it literally to the end of this book. Out of all the books at your disposal, you chose this one and I am forever thankful. You invested your time and energy into getting this far, and I hope, beyond a shadow of a doubt, it was time and energy well spent.

If you enjoyed the book, can you do me a fist bump solid? Please submit a review of book on Amazon. This allows other college students to more easily find this book and helps me refine and hone my writing to improve this and all future writing projects to come.

As always, you can reach me at:

cody@fearpunchingcody.com

All the best to you and your journey,

Cody Smith.

REFERENCES

The Permanent Detour: Underemployment's Long-Term Effects on the Careers of College Grads. (2018). *Burning Glass Technologies and Strada Institute for the Future of Work*. Retrieved from https://www.burning-glass.com/wp-content/uploads/permanent_detour_underemploym ent_report.pdf

Made in the USA
Monee, IL
14 January 2023

25173098R00083